PIANO · VOCAL · GUITAR
ULTIMATE

Classic Rock

70 GREAT HITS

ISBN 0-634-05543-7

HAL · LEONARD®
CORPORATION
7777 W. BLUEMOUND RD. P.O. BOX 13819 MILWAUKEE, WI 53213

Visit Hal Leonard Online at
www.halleonard.com

ULTIMATE Classic Rock

ALL RIGHT NOW

Words and Music by PAUL RODGERS
and ANDY FRASER

ANGIE

Words and Music by MICK JAGGER
and KEITH RICHARDS

BACK ON THE CHAIN GANG

Words and Music by
CHRISSIE HYNDE

Oh, _____

back on the chain___ gang.

Repeat and Fade

BADGE

Words and Music by ERIC CLAPTON
and GEORGE HARRISON

BEAST OF BURDEN

Words and Music by MICK JAGGER
and KEITH RICHARDS

BEHIND BLUE EYES

Words and Music by
PETE TOWNSHEND

BEST OF MY LOVE

Words and Music by JOHN DAVID SOUTHER,
DON HENLEY and GLENN FREY

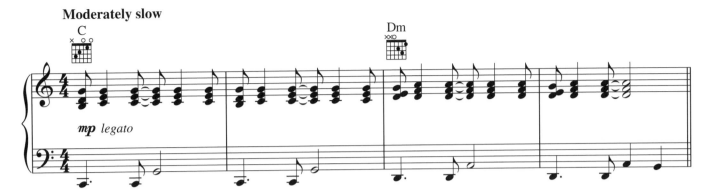

Ev-er-y night __ I'm ly-in' in bed, __ hold-in' you close __ in my
Beau-ti-ful fac-es and loud emp-ty plac-es, look at the way that we

dreams; __ think-in' a-bout __ all the things that we __ said __ and
live; __ wast-in' our time __ on cheap talk and wine

com - in' a - part ___ at the seams. ___ We try to talk it o -
left us so ___ lit - tle to give. ___ That same old crowd was like a

- ver but the words come out ___ too ___ rough;
cold dark cloud that words we could nev - er rise a - bove;

I know you were try - in' to give me the best ___ of your ___
but here in my heart ___ I give you the best ___ of my ___

love.
love.

Oh, _____ sweet dar -

BETH

Words and Music by PETER CRISS, BOB EZRIN
and STAN PENRIDGE

Rock Ballad, with feeling

Beth, I hear you call - in', but I can't come home right now.
You say you feel so emp - ty, that our house just ain't a home.

Me and the boys are play - in' and we just can't find the sound.
I'm al - ways some - where else and you're al - ways there a - lone.

BRAIN DAMAGE

Words and Music by
ROGER WATERS

BLACK MAGIC WOMAN

Words and Music by
PETER GREEN

BURNING FOR YOU

Words and Music by DONALD ROESER
and RICHARD MELTZER

Moderate Rock

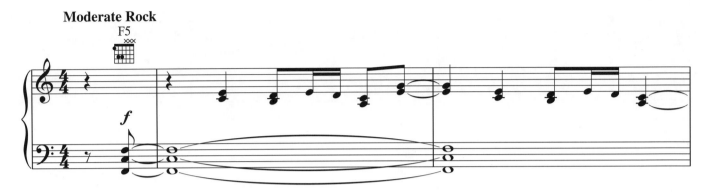

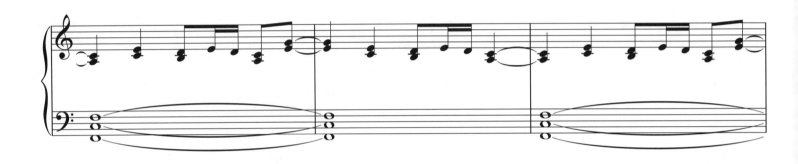

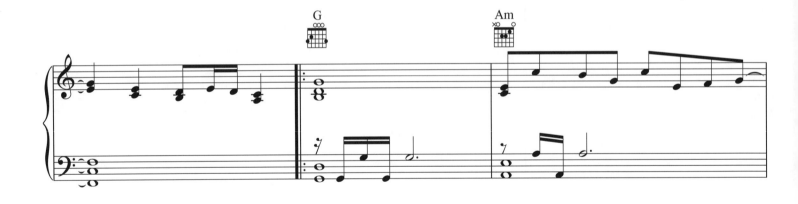

CALIFORNIA GIRLS

Words and Music by BRIAN WILSON
and MIKE LOVE

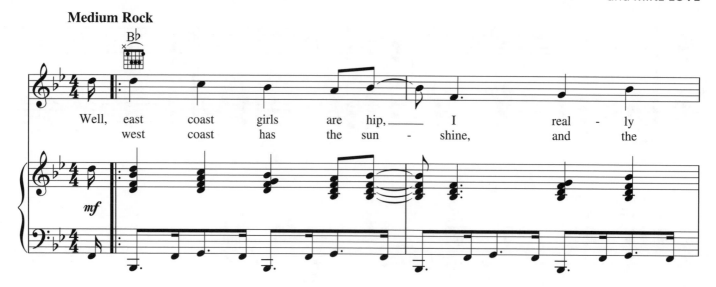

girls.

I

wish they all could be _____ Cal - i - for - nia, I

wish they all could be _____ Cal - i - for - nia, I

Repeat and Fade

COME SAIL AWAY

Words and Music by
DENNIS DeYOUNG

CRAZY LITTLE THING CALLED LOVE

Words and Music by
FREDDIE MERCURY

Oh, this thing ___ called ___ called

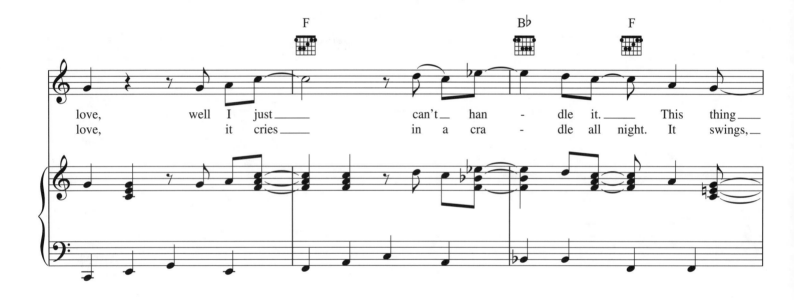

love, well I just ___ can't han - dle it. ___ This thing ___
love, it cries ___ in a cra - dle all night. It swings, ___

___ called love, I ___ must ___ get a
___ it jives, it shakes ___ all o - ver like a

mo - tor bike __ un - til I'm read - y.   Cra - y lit - tle thing called

love.

DON'T DO ME LIKE THAT

Words and Music by
TOM PETTY

(1.) I was talk - in' with a friend of mine, said a wom - an had hurt his pride.
(2., D.S.) Lis - ten hon - ey, can you see? Ba - by, it would bur - y me ___

DON'T LET THE SUN GO DOWN ON ME

Words and Music by ELTON JOHN
and BERNIE TAUPIN

DREAMER

Words and Music by RICK DAVIES
and ROGER HODGSON

Moderately fast

Dream - er, you know you are a dream - er. Well, can you put your hands in your head, oh no! I said dream - er, you're noth - ing but a

Can you put your hands   in your head,   oh   no!   Oh

no!

Fade out

Optional Ending

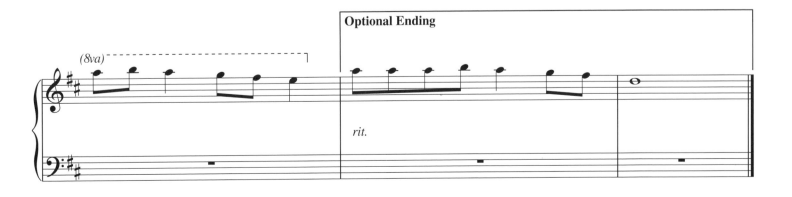

rit.

DUST IN THE WIND

Words and Music by
KERRY LIVGREN

EVERY LITTLE THING SHE DOES IS MAGIC

Music and Lyrics
STING

EYE IN THE SKY

Words and Music by ALAN PARSONS
and ERIC WOOLFSON

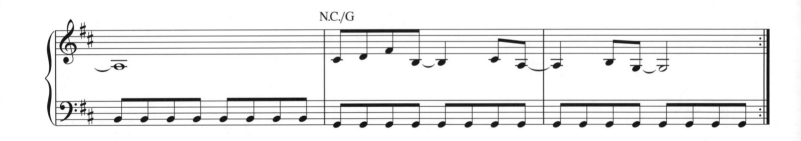

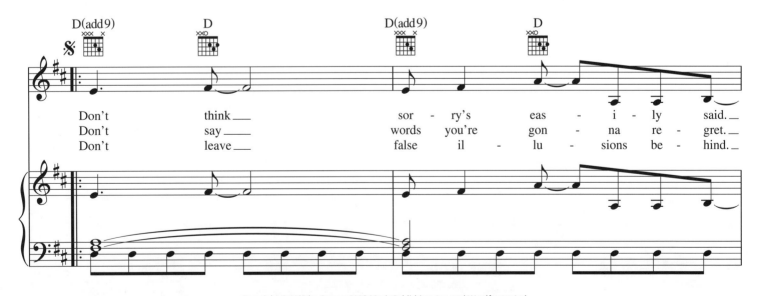

Don't think ___ sor - ry's eas - i - ly said.
Don't say ___ words you're gon - na re - gret.
Don't leave ___ false il - lu - sions be - hind.

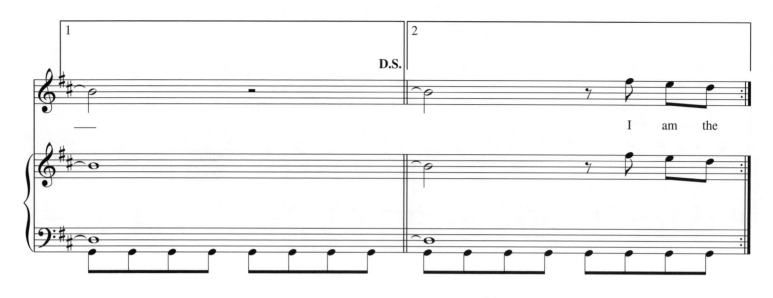

I am the

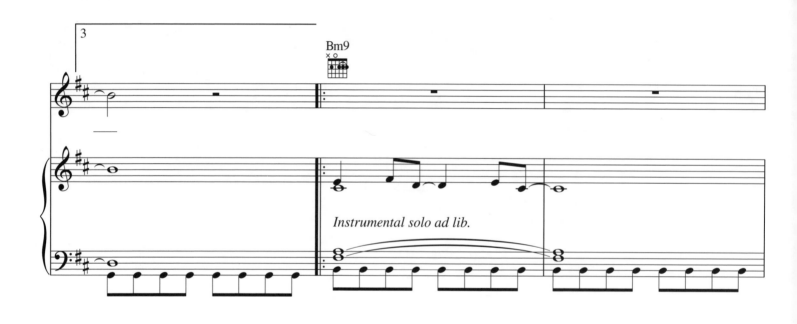

Instrumental solo ad lib.

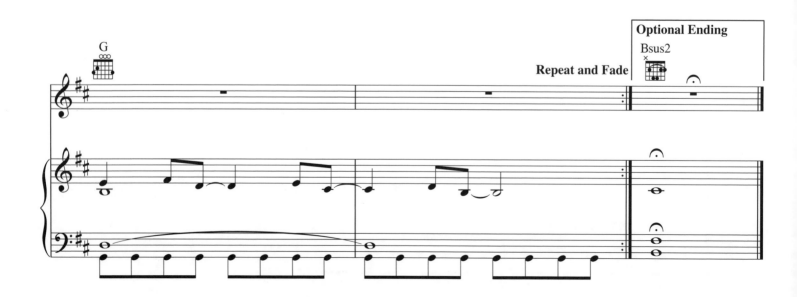

FIELDS OF GOLD

Music and Lyrics by
STING

Flowing, moderately

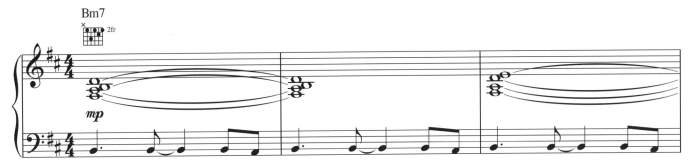

You'll re-mem-ber me, when the west wind moves___ up a-
stay with me, when will you be my love___ a-

on the fields___ of bar - ley. You'll for - get the sun in his
mong the fields___ of bar - ley? We'll for - get the sun in his

GIVE A LITTLE BIT

Words and Music by RICK DAVIES
and ROGER HODGSON

GOOD VIBRATIONS

Words and Music by BRIAN WILSON
and MIKE LOVE

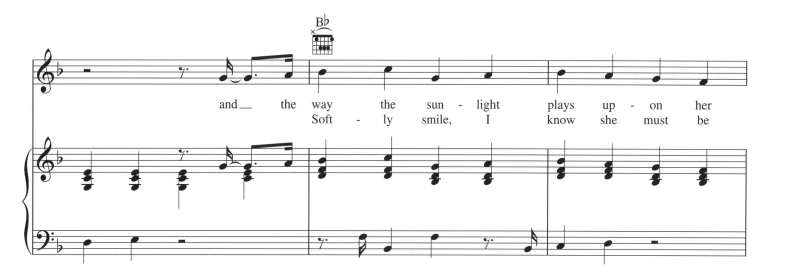

GREEN-EYED LADY

Words and Music by JERRY CORBETTA,
J.C. PHILLIPS and DAVID RIORDAN

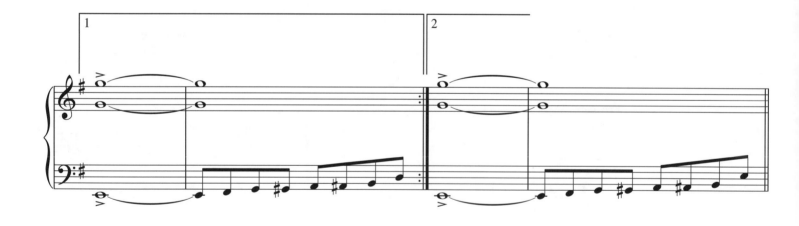

Green - Eyed La - dy, love - ly la - dy,

lone - ly lov - ers free. _____

Green - Eyed La - dy, wind - swept la - dy, _____

rules the night, _____ the waves, _____ the sand. ___

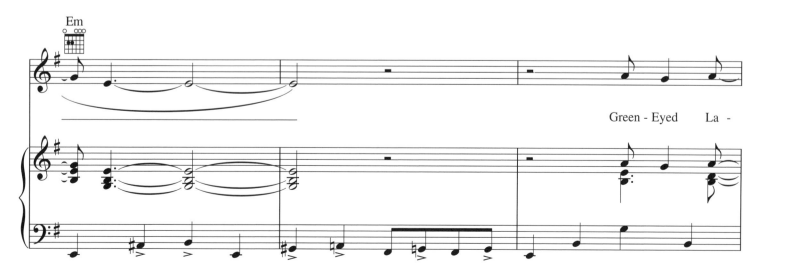

Green - Eyed La -

HARD HABIT TO BREAK

Words and Music by STEPHEN KIPNER
and JOHN LEWIS PARKER

Moderately slow

I guess I thought you'd be ___ here for - ev - er;
found some - one else; you had ___ ev - 'ry rea - son.

an - oth - er il - lu - sion I chose to cre - ate. ___ You
You know I can't blame you for run - nin' to him. ___ Two

HEAVEN

Words and Music by BRYAN ADAMS
and JIM VALLANCE

HUSH

Words and Music by
JOE SOUTH

Driving Rock

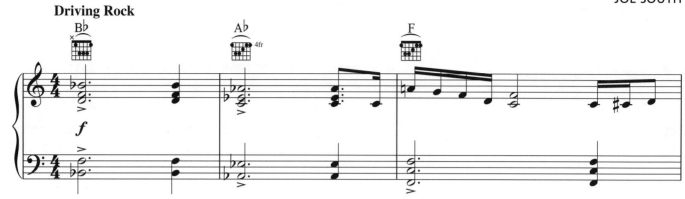

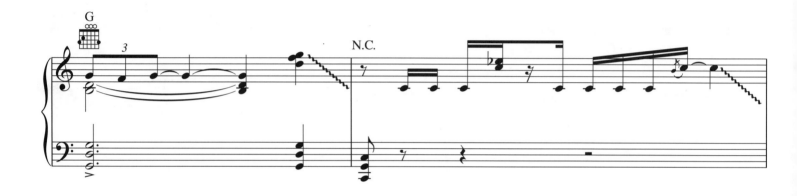

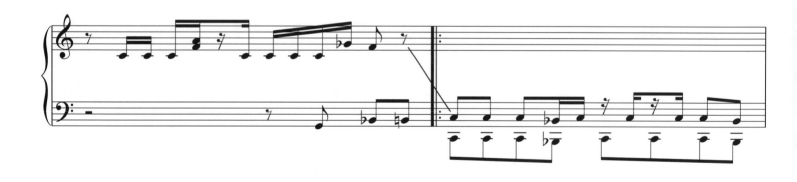

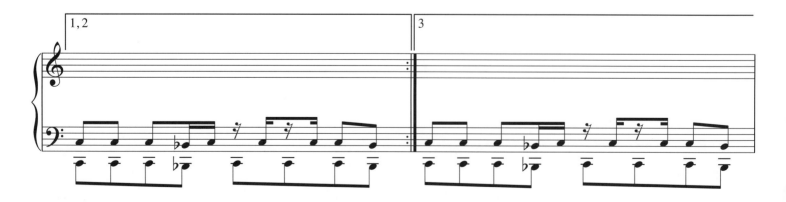

(Na, na na na, na na na, na na na.)

(Na, na na na, na na na, na na na.)

I got a

na,   na na   na.)

Instrumental break

Break ends

(Na,   na na

na,   na na na,   na na

na.)

LANDSLIDE

Words and Music by
STEVIE NICKS

I took my love ___ and I took it down. ___

I climbed a moun - tain and I ___ turned a - round. ___ And I

saw my ___ re - flec - tion in the snow - cov - ered hills ___ till the

I LOVE ROCK 'N ROLL

Words and Music by ALAN MERRILL
and JAKE HOOKER

I saw him danc-ing there___ by the rec-ord ma-
smiled, so I got up___ and asked___ for his

I WANT YOU TO WANT ME

Words and Music by
RICK NIELSEN

Bright Two-Beat

want   you   to want ___ me.   I

need   you   to need ___ me.   I'd

IT'S STILL ROCK AND ROLL TO ME

Words and Music by
BILLY JOEL

Moderately fast

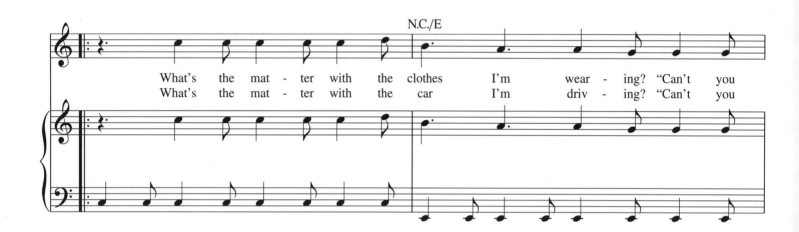

What's the mat - ter with the clothes I'm wear - ing? "Can't you
What's the mat - ter with the car I'm driv - ing? "Can't you

tell that your tie's too wide?"____
tell that it's out of style?"____

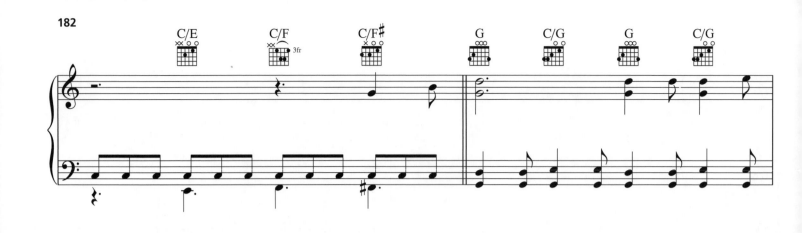

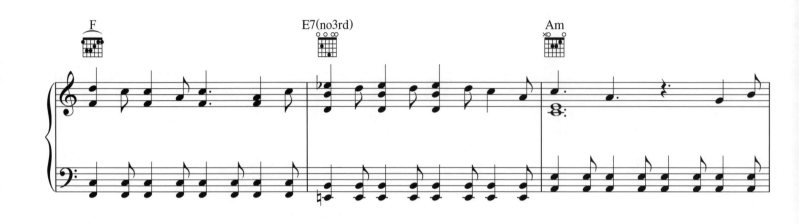

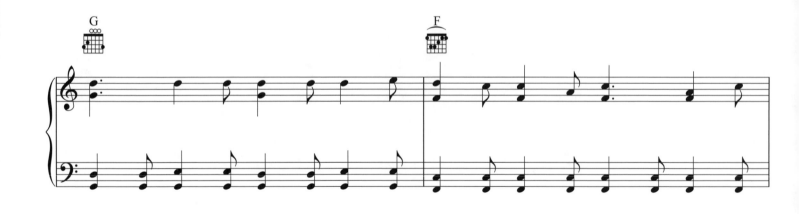

JOY TO THE WORLD

Words and Music by
HOYT AXTON

Moderate Gospel Rock

Je-re-mi-ah was a bull-frog, Was a good friend of
If I were the king of the world, Tell you what I'd do.
know I love la - dies, Love to have my fun.

mine.
Nev-er un-der-stood a sin-gle word he said,__ But I
Throw a-way the cars and the bars and the wars, And
I'm a high night fly-er and a rain-bow ri-der, A

helped him a-drink-in' his wine.__ Yes he al-ways had some might-y fine
make sweet love to you.__ Yes I'd make sweet love to
straight shoot-in' son-of-a-gun.__ Yes a straight shoot-in' son of a

LAY DOWN SALLY

Words and Music by ERIC CLAPTON,
MARCY LEVY and GEORGE TERRY

Bright beat

There is noth - ing that __ is wrong __ in want - ing you __ to stay __
sun ain't near - ly on __ the rise, __ and we still got __ the moon __
long to see __ the morn - ing light __ col - or - ing __ your face __

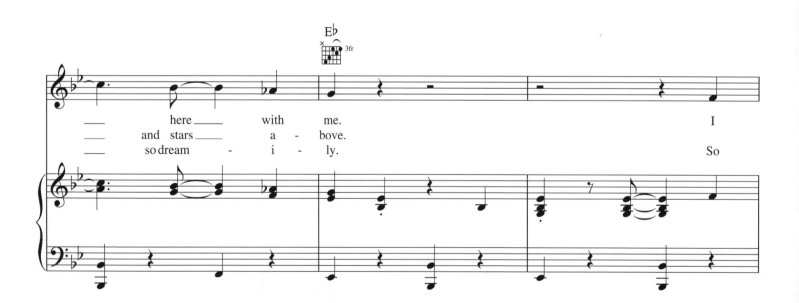

__ here __ with me.   I
__ and stars __ a - bove.
__ so dream - i - ly.   So

LIGHTS

Words and Music by STEVE PERRY
and NEAL SCHON

my, my, my, my, oh, oh,

2nd time D.S. al Coda

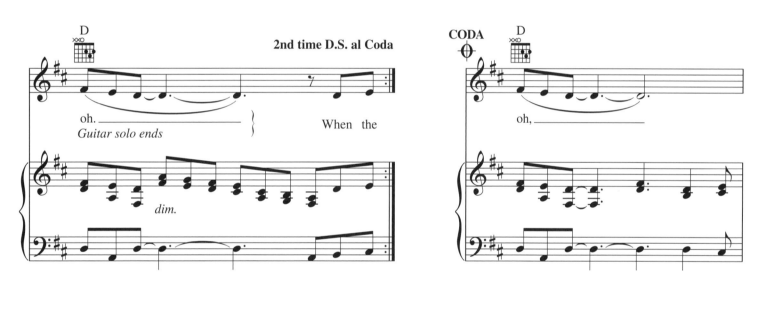

oh.
Guitar solo ends
dim.
When the

CODA

oh,

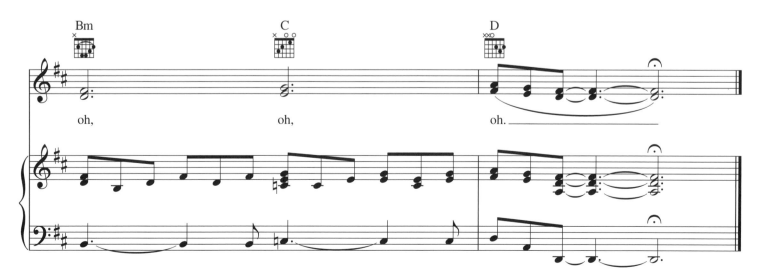

oh, oh, oh.

LIGHT MY FIRE

Words and Music by
THE DOORS

LIVIN' ON A PRAYER

Words and Music by DESMOND CHILD,
JON BON JOVI and RICHIE SAMBORA

Moderate Rock

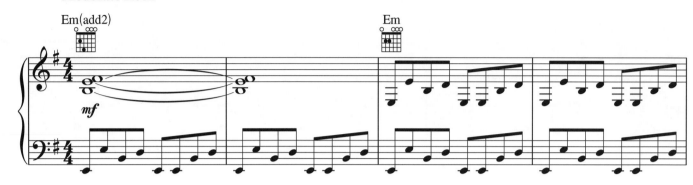

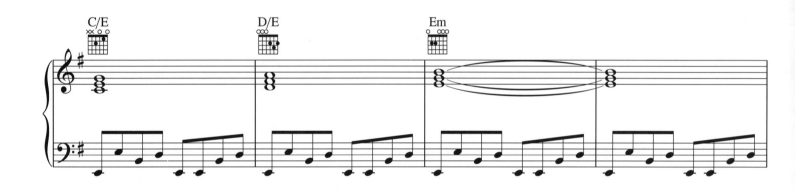

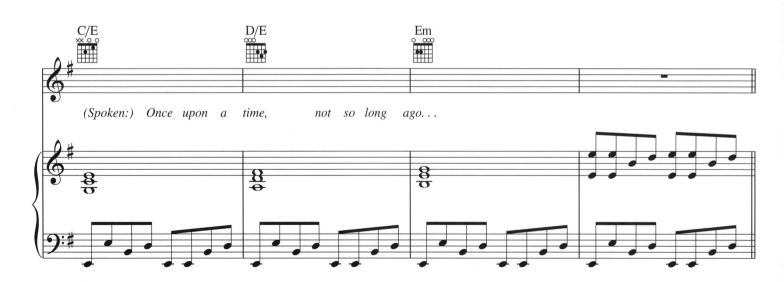

(Spoken:) Once upon a time, not so long ago...

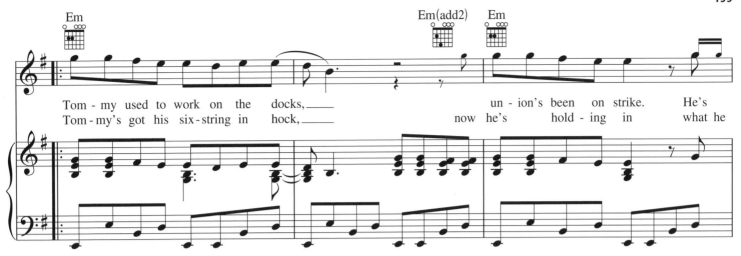

Tom - my used to work on the docks,_____ un - ion's been on strike. He's
Tom - my's got his six - string in hock,_____ now he's hold - ing in what he

down on his luck, it's tough,_____ so tough.__
used to make it talk. So tough,_____ it's tough.__

_____ Gi - na works the di - ner all day____
_____ Gi - na dreams of run - ning a - way;____

MONY, MONY

Words and Music by BOBBY BLOOM,
TOMMY JAMES, RITCHIE CORDELL
and BO GENTRY

Here she comes now, say, Mo - ny, Mo - ny.____
Wake me, shake me, Mo - ny, Mo - ny.____

Shoot 'em down, turn a - round,
Shot - gun git it done,

come on, Mo - ny.____
come on, Mo - ny.____

ONE THING LEADS TO ANOTHER

Words and Music by CY CURNIN, JAMIE WEST-ORAM,
ADAM WOODS, RUPERT GREENALL
and ALFRED AGIUS

The de - cep - tion with tact; just
- sion that you sell
- sy to be - lieve

what are you try - ing to say?___ You got a black face which
pass - es in and out like a scent.___ But the long face
some - bod - y's been ly - ing to me.___ But when the wrong word goes in the

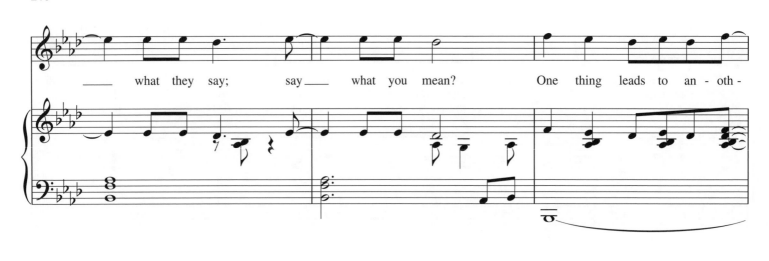

_____ what they say; say _____ what you mean? One thing leads to an - oth -

- er. You told me some - thing wrong; I know I lis - ten too long, _____ but then

To Coda ⊕

1

one thing leads to an - oth - er.

2

The im - pres - - er, yeah, yeah, yeah.

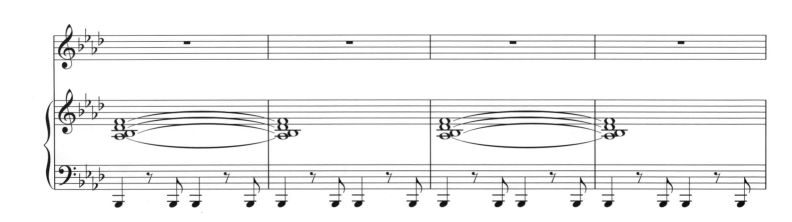

One thing   one thing leads to an - oth - er. ___

D.S. al Coda

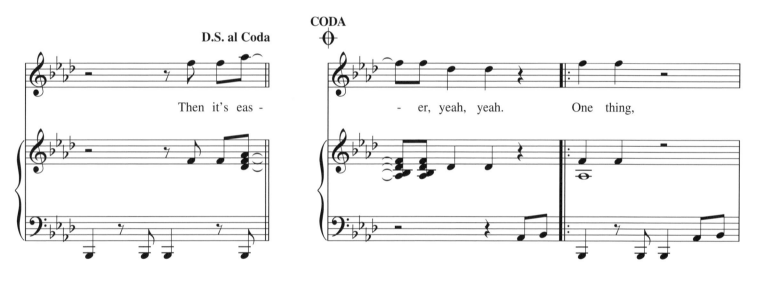

Then it's eas -

CODA

- er, yeah, yeah.   One thing,

one thing leads to an - oth - er. ___

Repeat and Fade   **Optional Ending**

PAPERBACK WRITER

Words and Music by JOHN LENNON
and PAUL McCARTNEY

Bright Rock

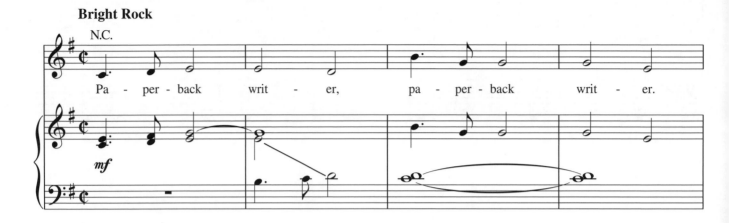

Pa - per - back writ - er, pa - per - back writ - er.

Dear __ Sir or Mad - am, will you read my book? It took me
It's a thou - sand pag - es, give or take a few, I'll be

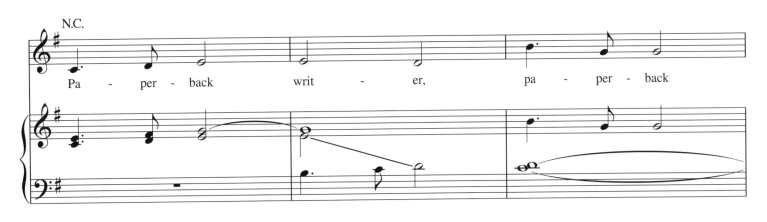

Pa - per - back writ - er, pa - per - back

writ - er.

Pa - per - back

Repeat and Fade

writ - er.

PARADISE BY THE DASHBOARD LIGHT

Words and Music by
JIM STEINMAN

BASEBALL PLAY-BY-PLAY ON THE CAR RADIO

O.K., here we go, we got a real pressure cooker going here, two down, nobody on, no score, bottom of the ninth, there's the wind up, and there it is, a line shot up the middle, look at him go. This boy can really fly!

He's rounding first and really turning it on now, he's not letting up at all, he's gonna try for second; the ball is bobbled out in center, and here comes the throw, and what a throw! He's gonna slide in head first, here he comes, he's out! No, wait safe-safe at second base, this kid really makes things happen out there.

Batter steps up to the plate, here's the pitch-he's going, and what a jump he's got, he's trying for third, here's the throw, it's in the dirt-safe at third! Holy cow, stolen base!

He's taking a pretty big lead out there, almost daring him to try and pick him off. The pitcher glances over, winds up, and it's bunted, bunted down the third base line, the suicide squeeze is on! Here he comes, squeeze play, it's gonna be close, here's the throw, here's the play at the plate, holy cow, I think he's gonna make it!

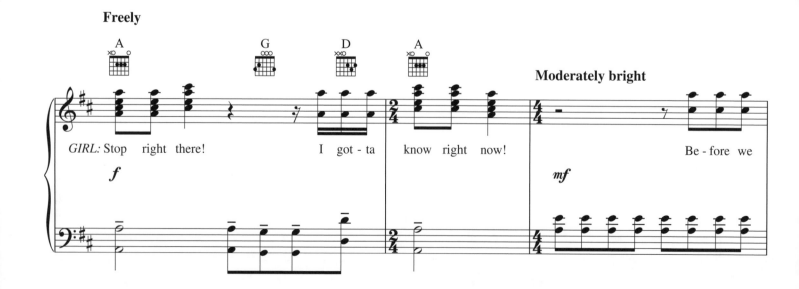

make me so hap-py for the rest of my life?_ Will you take me a-way_ and will you

make me your wife?_ I got-ta know right now! Be-fore we

go an-y fur-ther, do you love me? Will you love me for-ev- er?

(Spoken:) What's it gonna be, boy? Come on! I can wait all night!

What's it gonna be, boy... yes or no? What's it gonna be, boy? Yes...

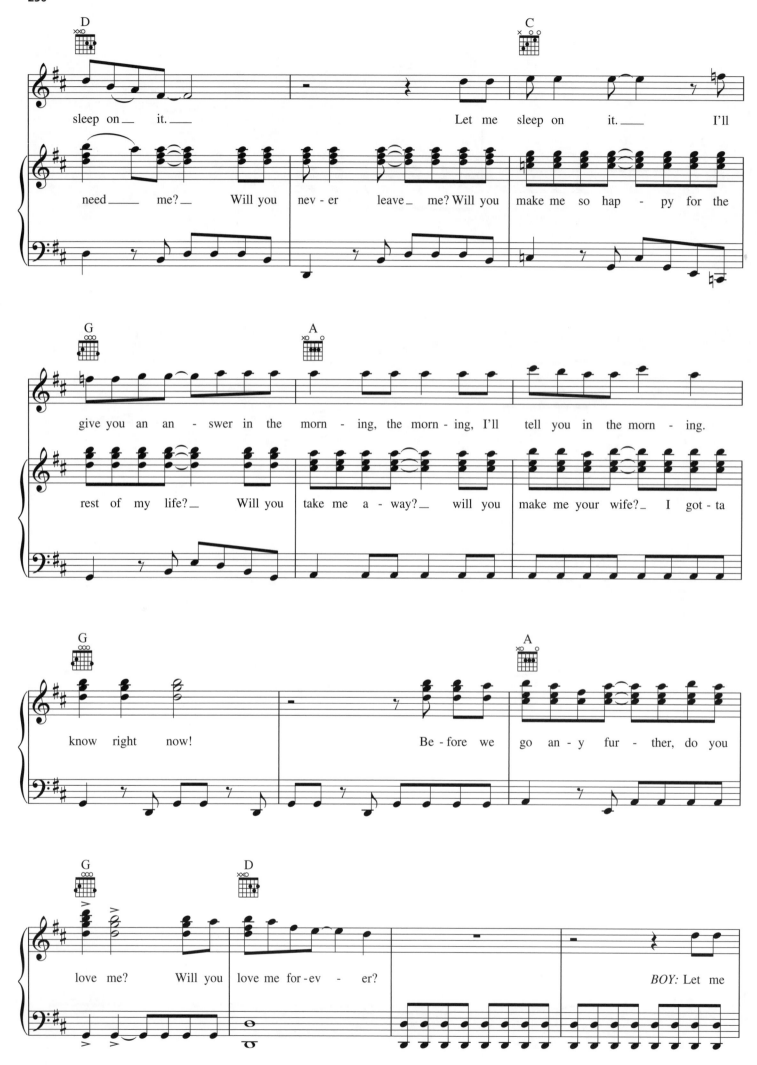

RAMBLIN' MAN

Words and Music by
DICKEY BETTS

Repeat and Fade

PIECE OF MY HEART

Words and Music by BERT BERNS
and JERRY RAGOVOY

Slowly, with a beat

mf

Did - n't I make you feel like you were the on - ly man, ___ did - n't I give you ev - 'ry - thing that a wom - an pos - si - bly can? ___

PINBALL WIZARD

Words and Music by
PETE TOWNSHEND

PINK HOUSES

Words and Music by
JOHN MELLENCAMP

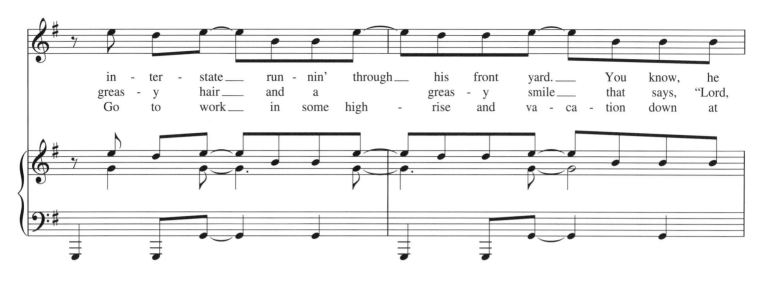

in - ter - state___ run - nin' through___ his front yard.___ You know, he
greas - y hair___ and a greas - y smile___ that says, "Lord,
Go to work___ in some high - rise and va - ca - tion down at

thinks he's got it so good.___ And there's a
this must be my des - ti - na - tion." 'Cause they
the Gulf of Mex - i - co.___ And there's

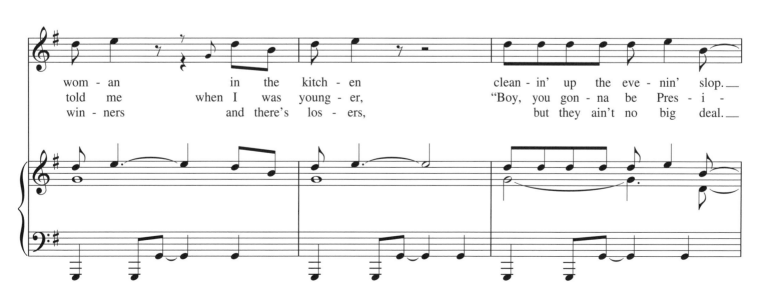

wom - an in the kitch - en clean - in' up the eve - nin' slop.___
told me when I was young - er, "Boy, you gon - na be Pres - i -
win - ners and there's los - ers, but they ain't no big deal.___

RADAR LOVE

Words and Music by GEORGE KOOYMANS
and BARRY HAY

Slowly

Driving shuffle

1,2,3

4

I've been driv - in' all night. My hand's wet on the wheel.
ra - di - o was play - in' some for - got - ten song.
No more speed, I'm al - most there.

There's a voice in my head that
Bren - da Lee is
I got - ta keep cool now, I

drives my heel.___ It's my ba -
com - in' on strong.___ The road___
got - ta take care.___ Last___

- by call - in', said, "I need___ you here."___
___ has got___ me hyp - no - tized.___
___ car to pass, here___ I go.___

And it's half past four and I'm shift - in' gear.___
And I'll be spit - ting in - to a new sun - rise.___
And the line of cars drove down real slow.___

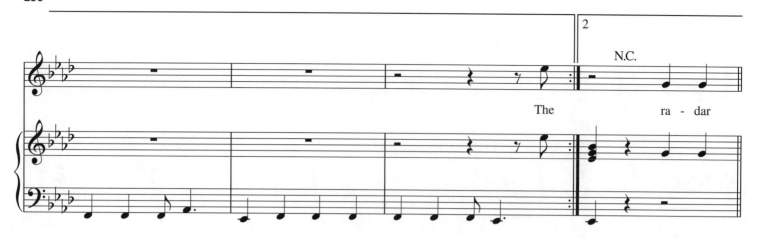

The   ra - dar

Play 4 times

love._

N.C.

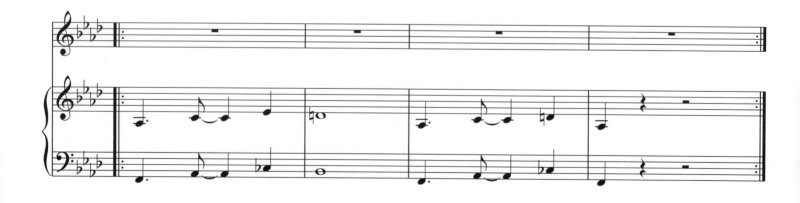

that's called _____ ra - dar love.__

REVOLUTION

Words and Music by JOHN LENNON
and PAUL McCARTNEY

Moderate Rock and Roll Shuffle

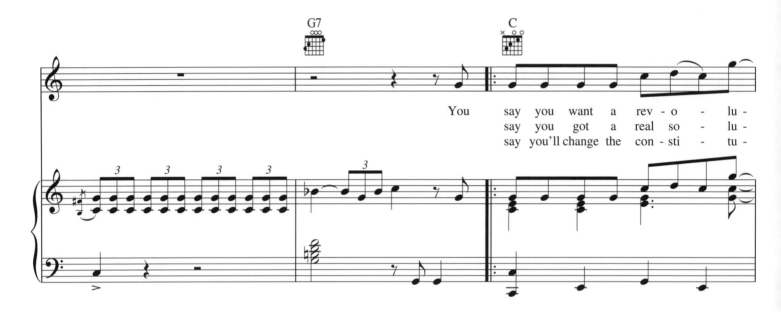

You say you want a rev-o-lu-
say you got a real so-lu-
say you'll change the con-sti-tu-

-tion; _____ well, _____ you know, _____ we all want _____
-tion; _____ well, _____ you know, _____ we'd all love _____
-tion; _____ well, _____ you know, _____ we all want

ROCK THIS TOWN

Words and Music by
BRIAN SETZER

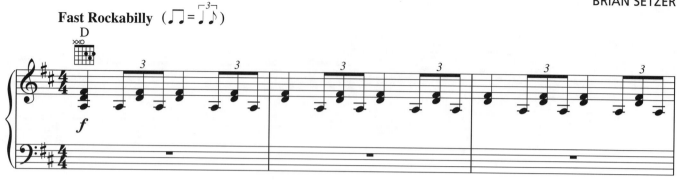

Well, my ba - by and me ___ went out ___ late Sat - ur - day night. ___
found a lit - tle place that real - ly did - n't look half
hav - in' a ball ___ just a - bop - pin' on the big dance

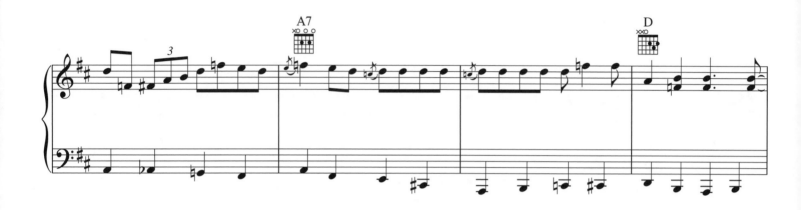

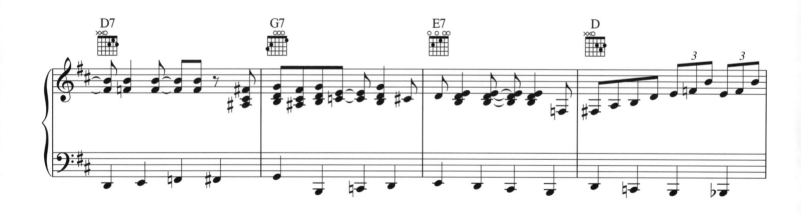

Solo ends

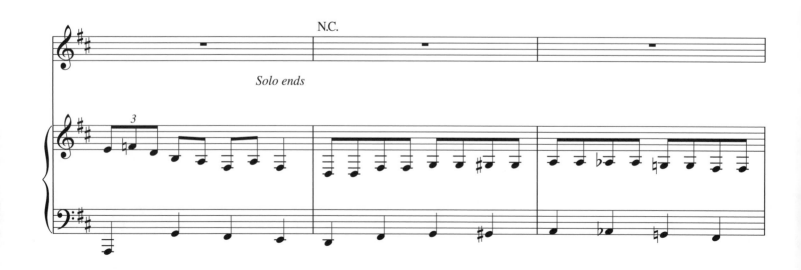

SAY YOU WILL

Words and Music by MICK JONES
and LOU GRAMM

With a beat

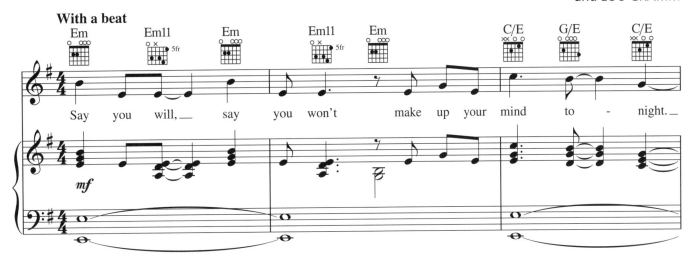

Say you will, — say you won't make up your mind to - night. —

— Say you do, — say you don't wan - na be mine. —

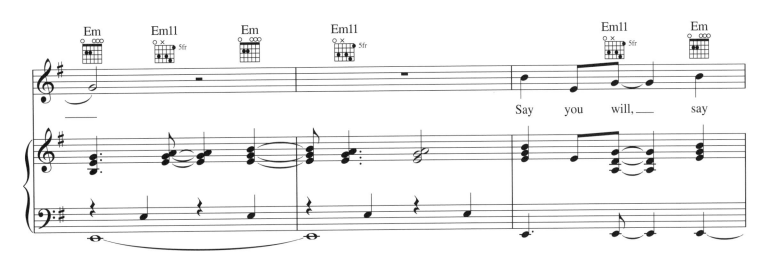

Say you will, — say

ROLL WITH THE CHANGES

Words and Music by
KEVIN CRONIN

As soon as you are a-

-ble,_____ wom - an, I____ am will - ing to make

-pen,_____ felt the ta - bles turn - in'.

SEPARATE WAYS
(Worlds Apart)

Words and Music by STEVE PERRY
and JONATHAN CAIN

Moderately fast Rock

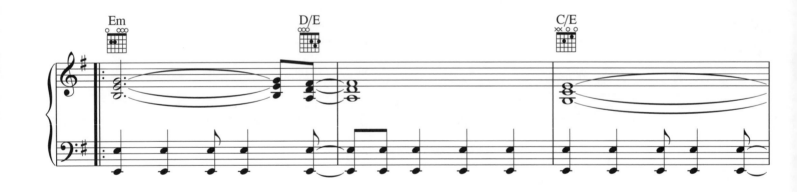

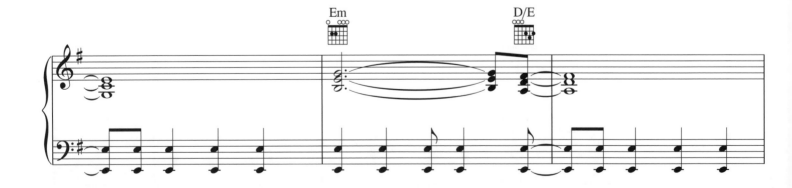

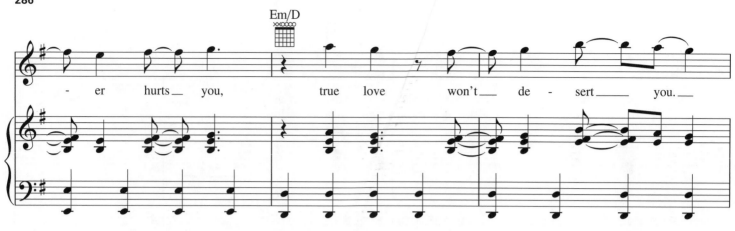

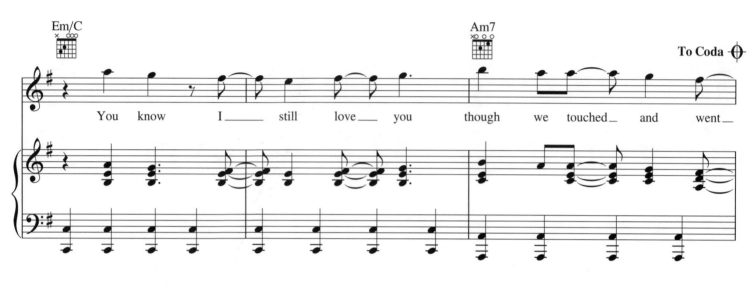

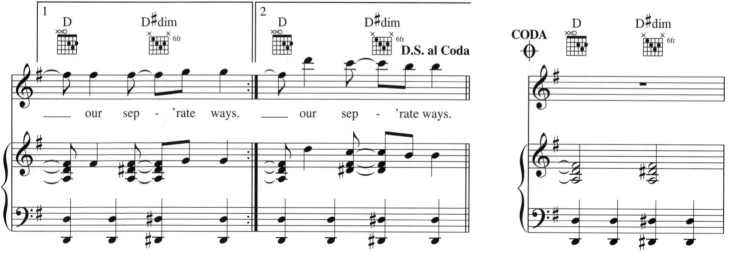

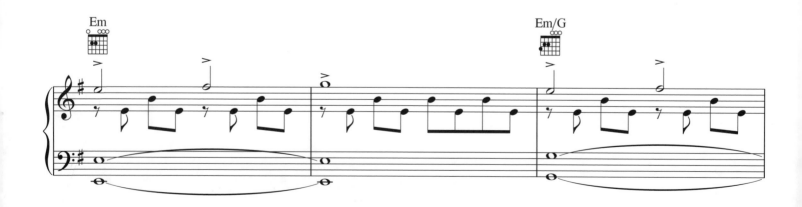

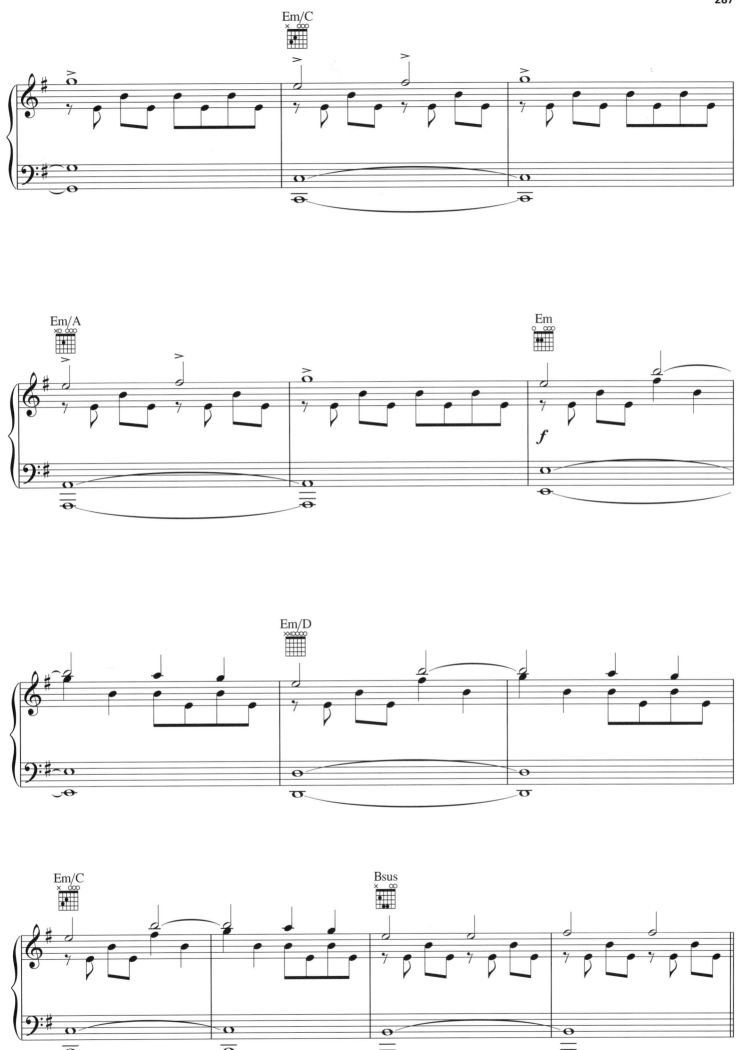

SISTER CHRISTIAN

Words and Music by
KELLY KEAGY

SMALL TOWN

Words and Music by
JOHN MELLENCAMP

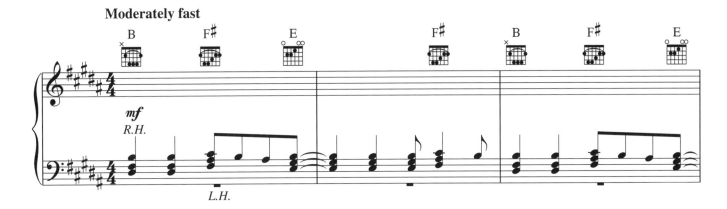

Well, I was born in a small ____ town,
Ed-u-cat-ed in ____ a small ____ town,

and I live in a small ____ town;
taught the fear of Je-sus in a small town;

prob-'ly die in a small ____
used to day-dream in that

(She's)
SOME KIND OF WONDERFUL

Words and Music by
JOHN ELLISON

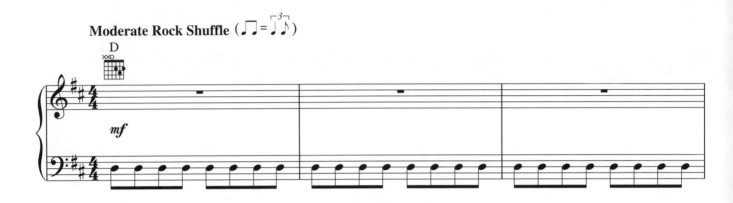

man could want. I got more____ than I could ask____
es me____ my heart be-comes filled with ___ de-

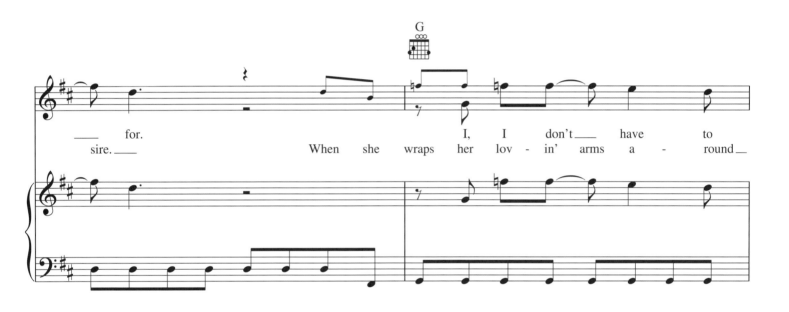

____ for. I, I don't____ have to
sire.____ When she wraps her lov-in' arms a - round____

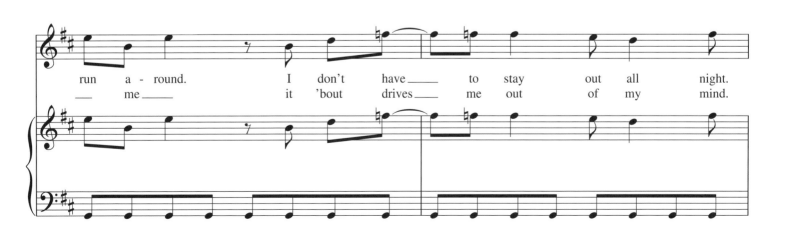

run a-round. I don't have____ to stay out all night.
____ me____ it 'bout drives____ me out of my mind.

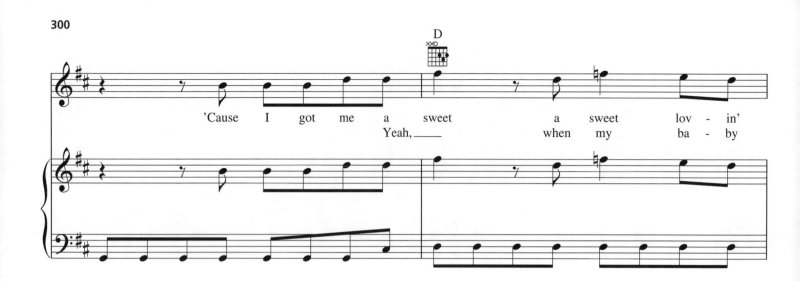

'Cause I got me a sweet   a sweet lov - in'
Yeah,___   when my   ba - by

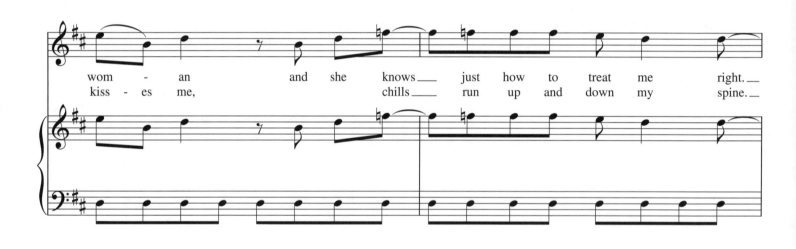

wom - an   and she knows___ just how to treat me   right.___
kiss - es me,   chills___ run up and down my   spine.___

Well my ba - by,   she's al - right.

a, got a sweet__ lit - tle wom - an like mine. Yeah.

Now can I get a wit - ness? Can I get a

wit - ness? Well, can I get a

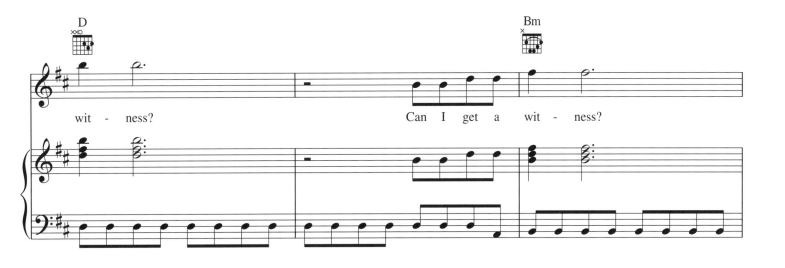

wit - ness? Can I get a wit - ness?

STAGES

Words and Music by BILLY F GIBBONS,
DUSTY HILL and FRANK BEARD

It's a fine time to fall ___
Then you left me stand -
Now you're back and say ___

___ in love ___ with you. ___
- ing all ___ a - lone. ___
___ you're gon - na stay. ___

I ___
I could -
I would -

that I ___ was gone. ___
you had ___ to go? ___
to come ___ and go. ___

Stag - es ___ keep ___ on chang - ing. Stag - es ___ re -

- ar - rang - ing love. ___

Guitar solo ad lib.

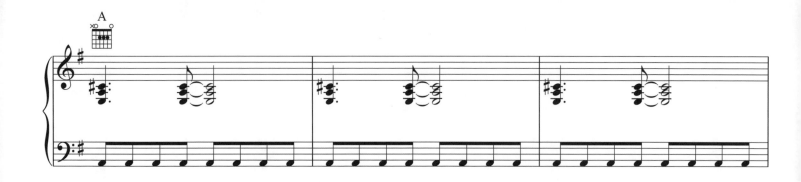

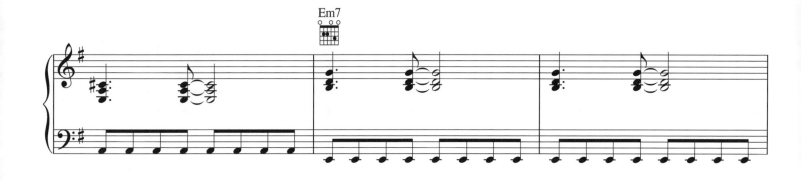

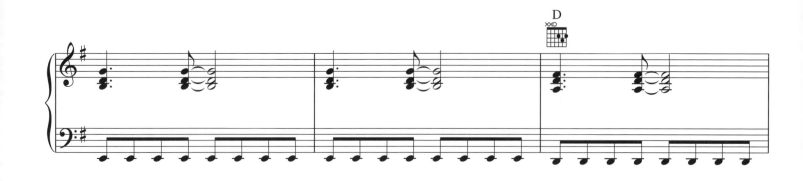

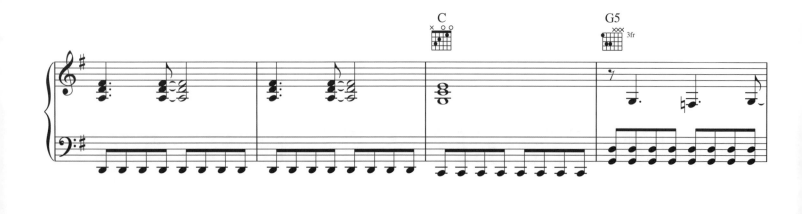

SUITE: JUDY BLUE EYES

Words and Music by
STEPHEN STILLS

Chest - nut - brown — ca - nar — — y, _____ ru - by throat - ed spar -
Voic - es of _____ the an — gels, _____ ring a - round _ the moon -
Lac - y, lilt - ing lyr - ic, _____ los - ing love, _ la - ment -

D/E   E   A/E

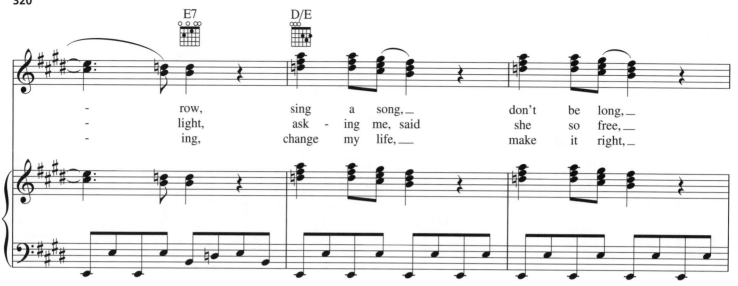

Do do do do do, do do do do do do, do do do do do, do do do do.

(So)
TIRED OF WAITING FOR YOU

Words and Music by
RAY DAVIES

SULTANS OF SWING

Words and Music by
MARK KNOPFLER

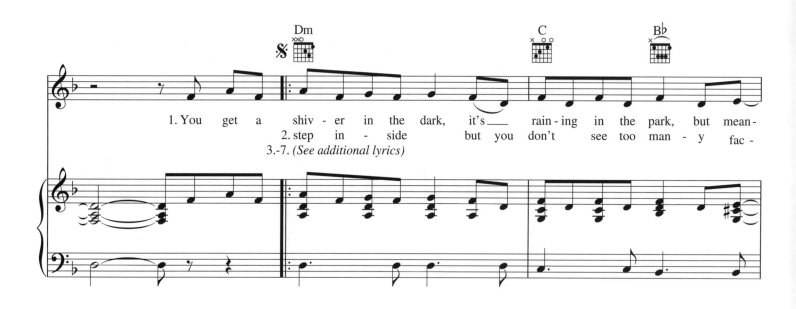

1. You get a shiv - er in the dark, it's ___ rain - ing in the park, but mean -
2. step in - side but you don't see too man - y fac -
3.-7. *(See additional lyrics)*

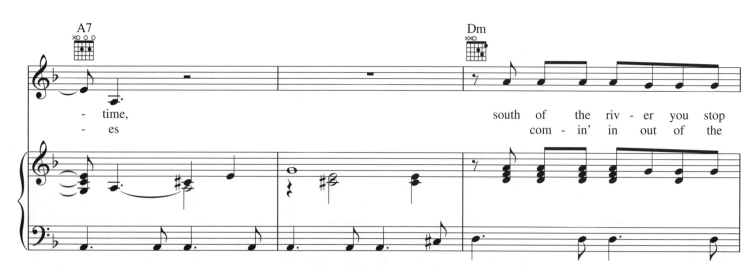

- time,
- es

south of the riv - er you stop
com - in' in out of the

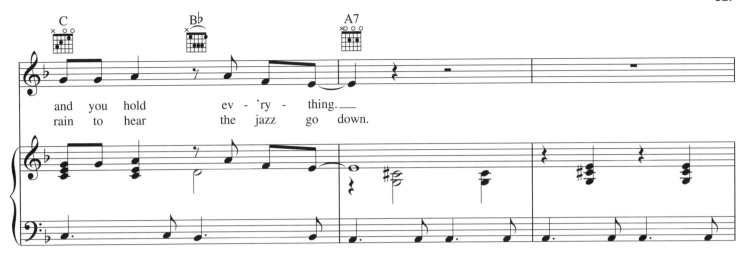

and you hold ev - 'ry - thing. ___
rain to hear the jazz go down.

A band is blow - in' Dix - ie dou - ble four ___ time.
Too much com - pe - ti - tion, too man - y oth - er plac - es,

You feel all right when you hear that mu - sic ring. ___
but not too man - y horns can make that

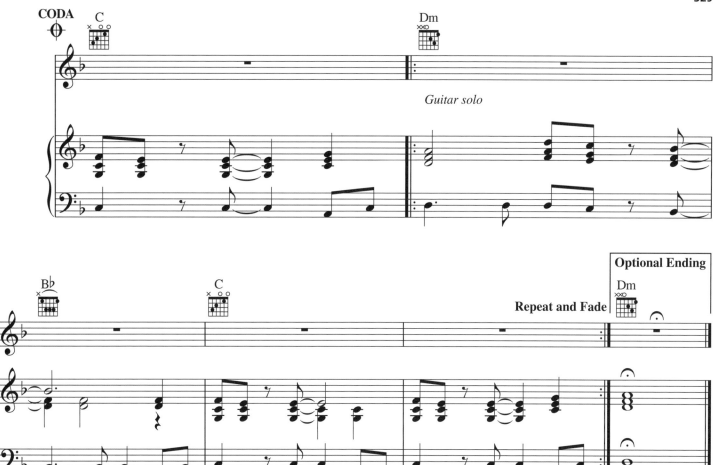

Guitar solo

Additional Lyrics

3. You can check out Guitar George, he knows all the chords.
   Mind you, he's strictly rhythm, he doesn't want to make it cry or sing.
   An old guitar is all he can afford,
   When he gets up under the lights, to play his thing.

4. And Harry doesn't mind if he doesn't make the scene.
   He's got a daytime job and he's doin' all right.
   He can play honky-tonk just like anything,
   Savin' it up for Friday night
   With the Sultans, with the Sultans of Swing.

5. And a crowd of young boys, they're foolin' around in the corner,
   Drunk and dressed in their best brown baggies and their platform soles.
   They don't give a damn about any trumpet playin' band;
   It ain't what they call rock and roll.
   And the Sultans of Swing played Creole.

6. *Instrumental*

7. And then The Man, he steps right up to the microphone
   And says, at last, just as the time-bell rings:
   "Thank you, good night, now it's time to go home."
   And he makes it fast with one more thing:
   "We are the Sultans of Swing."

(To Coda)

SWEET EMOTION

Words and Music by STEVEN TYLER
and TOM HAMILTON

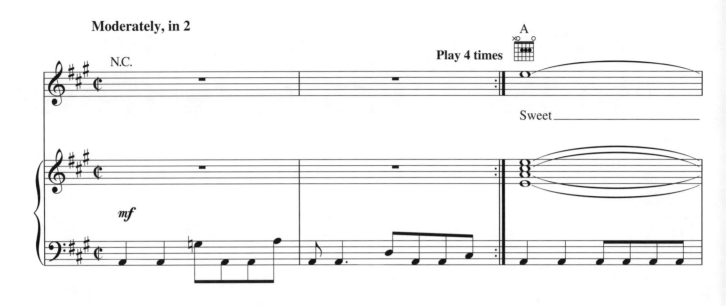

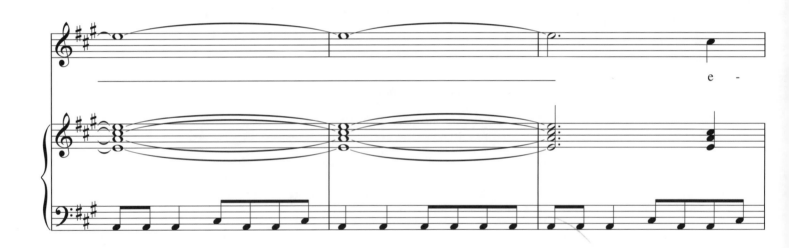

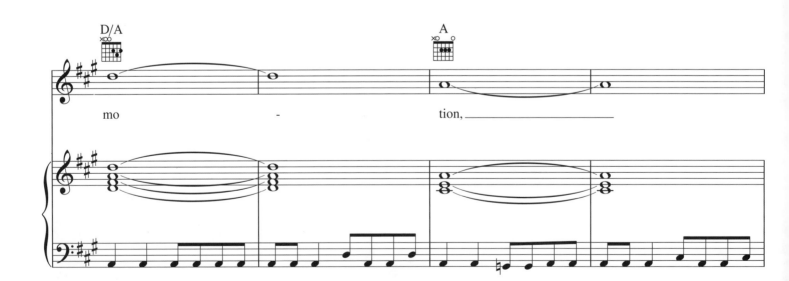

You're call - in' my name but I
Well, I got good news, she's a
You're tell - in' her things but your
I'm talk - in' 'bout some - thin' you can

got - ta make clear_____ I
real good li - ar,
girl - friend lied;_____ you
sure un - der - stand,_____ 'cause a

can't say, ba - by, where I'll be in a year._____
back - stage boo - gie set your pants on fire._____
can't catch me 'cause the rab - bit done died._____
month on the road and I'll be eat - in' from your hand._____

SWEET TALKIN' WOMAN

Words and Music by
JEFF LYNNE

Sweet talk-in' wom-an,
where did you go? _____ I was

search-in' on a one-way street, _____ I was hop-in' for a
walk-in' man-y days go by, _____ I was think-in' 'bout the
liv-in' on a dead-end street, _____ I've been ask-in' ev-'ry-

TAKIN' CARE OF BUSINESS

Words and Music by
RANDY BACHMAN

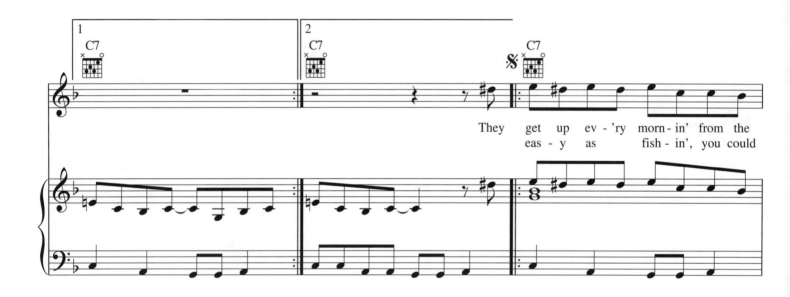

They get up ev-'ry morn-in' from the
eas-y as fish-in', you could

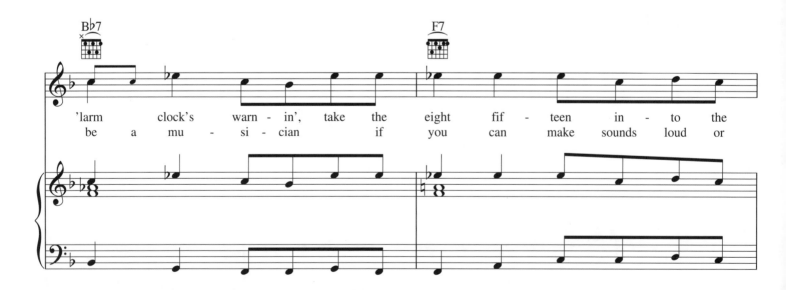

'larm clock's warn-in', take the eight fif-teen in-to the
be a mu-si-cian if you can make sounds loud or

cit - y. / mel - low. There's a whis - tle up a - bove and peo - ple / Get a sec - ond - hand gui - tar_____ chanc - es

push - in', peo - ple shov - in' and the girls who try to look / are you'll go_____ far. If you get in with the right bunch of

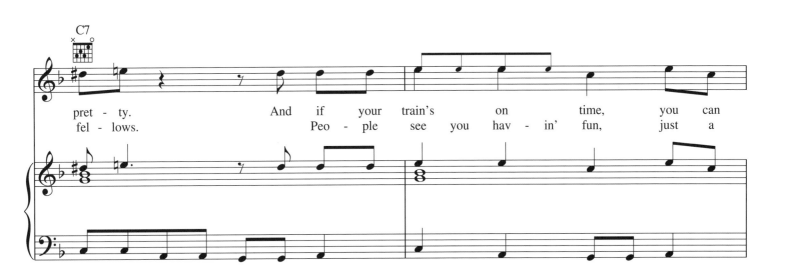

pret - ty. / fel - lows. And if your train's on time, you can / Peo - ple see you hav - in' fun, just a

get to work by nine, and start your slav - in' job to get your
ly - in' in the sun. Tell them that you like it this way.

pay. If you ev - er get an - noyed look at
It's the work that we a - void look and we're

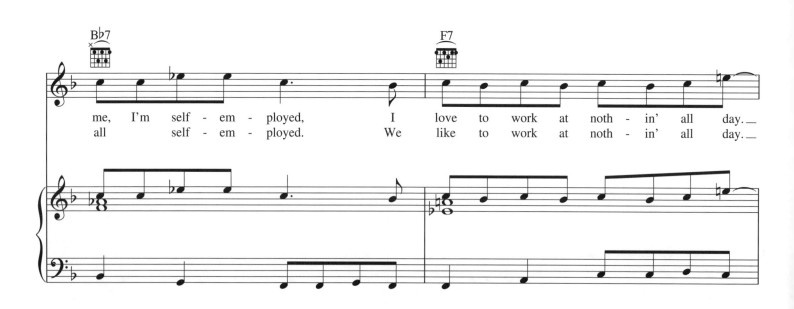

me, I'm self - em - ployed, I love to work at noth - in' all day.
all self - em - ployed. We like to work at noth - in' all day.

THROWING IT ALL AWAY

Words and Music by TONY BANKS,
PHIL COLLINS and MIKE RUTHERFORD

Need I say __ I love __ you
can - not live __ to - geth - er,
Some - day you'll __ be sor - ry.

need I say __ I care? __
we can - not live __ a - part. __
Some - day when __ you're free __

Need I say __ that e - mo - tion's
That's the sit - u - a - tion; I've
mem - o - ries will __ re - mind you that

some - thing we __ don't share? __
known it from __ the start. __
our love was meant __ to be __

TURN ME LOOSE

Words and Music by PAUL DEAN
and DUKE RENO

TWO AGAINST NATURE

Words and Music by WALTER BECKER
and DONALD FAGEN

Soak the tim - ber ___ with spe - cial spray. Nuke the it - ty bit - ty ones right

where they lay. Whip the bas - tards while they still green.

Ab7#9

Take the fire - mop; sweep it kiss-ing clean.

Repeat and Fade

VICTIM OF LOVE

Words and Music by JOHN DAVID SOUTHER,
DON HENLEY, GLENN FREY and DON FELDER

What kind of love ____ have you got? ____
Some peo - ple nev - er come clean. ____

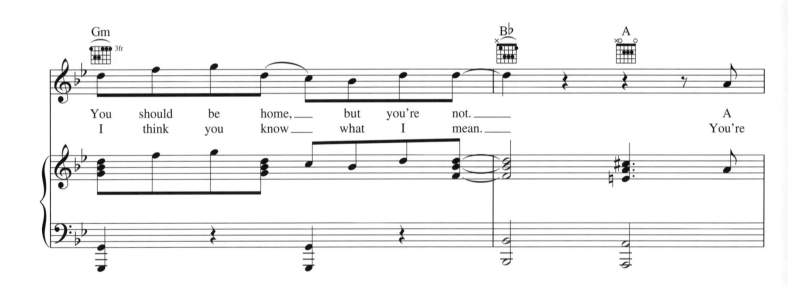

You should be home, ____ but you're not. ____ A
I think you know ____ what I mean. ____ You're

room full of noise ____ and dan - ger - ous boys
walk - in' the wire, ____ pain and de - sire,

WALKING IN MEMPHIS

Words and Music by
MARC COHN

WEREWOLVES OF LONDON

Words and Music by WARREN ZEVON,
ROBERT WACHTEL and LeROY MARINEL

kitch - en door.___ You bet - ter not let him in!___

Lit - tle old la - dy got mu - ti - la - ted

late last ___ night; ___ were - wolves of Lon - don ___ a - gain.

Ow - ooh! Were - wolves of Lon - don.___

Instrumental solo

A WHITER SHADE OF PALE

Words and Music by KEITH REID
and GARY BROOKER

We skipped the light____ fan - dan - go,____
She said, "I'm home____ on shore leave,"____
She said, "There is____ no rea - son,____

WONDERFUL TONIGHT

Words and Music by
ERIC CLAPTON

ZIGGY STARDUST

Words and Music by
DAVID BOWIE

YOU'RE IN MY HEART

Words and Music by
ROD STEWART

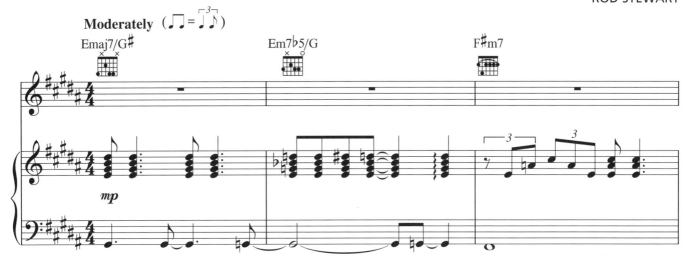

I did-n't know___ what day it was___ when you walked___
I took all___ those hab-its of yours that in the be-

THE ULTIMATE SERIES

This comprehensive series features jumbo collections of piano/vocal arrangements with guitar chords. Each volume features an outstanding selection of your favorite songs. Collect them all for the ultimate music library!

Blues

90 blues classics, including: Boom Boom • Born Under a Bad Sign • Gee Baby, Ain't I Good to You • I Can't Quit You Baby • Pride and Joy • (They Call It) Stormy Monday • Sweet Home Chicago • Why I Sing the Blues • You Shook Me • and more.
00310723 . . . .$19.95

Broadway Gold

100 show tunes: Beauty and the Beast • Do-Re-Mi • I Whistle a Happy Tune • The Lady Is a Tramp • Memory • My Funny Valentine • Oklahoma • Some Enchanted Evening • Summer Nights • Tomorrow • many more.
00361396 . . . .$21.95

Broadway Platinum

100 popular Broadway show tunes, featuring: Consider Yourself • Getting to Know You • Gigi • Do You Hear the People Sing • I'll Be Seeing You • My Favorite Things • People • She Loves Me • Try to Remember • Younger Than Springtime • many more.
00311496 . . . .$19.95

Children's Songbook

66 fun songs for kids: Alphabet Song • Be Our Guest • Bingo • The Brady Bunch • Do-Re-Mi • Hakuna Matata • It's a Small World • Kum Ba Yah • Sesame Street Theme • Tomorrow • Won't You Be My Neighbor? • and more.
00310690 . . . .$18.95

Christmas – Third Edition

Includes: Carol of the Bells • Deck the Hall • Frosty the Snow Man • Gesu Bambino • Good King Wenceslas • Jingle-Bell Rock • Joy to the World • Nuttin' for Christmas • O Holy Night • Rudolph the Red-Nosed Reindeer • Silent Night • What Child Is This? • and more.
00361399 . . . .$19.95

Country – Second Edition

90 of your favorite country hits: Boot Scootin' Boogie • Chattahoochie • Could I Have This Dance • Crazy • Down at the Twist And Shout • Hey, Good Lookin' • Lucille • When She Cries • and more.
00310036 . . . .$19.95

Gospel – 100 Songs of Devotion

Includes: El Shaddai • His Eye Is on the Sparrow • How Great Thou Art • Just a Closer Walk With Thee • Lead Me, Guide Me • (There'll Be) Peace in the Valley (For Me) • Precious Lord, Take My Hand • Wings of a Dove • more.
00241009 . . . .$19.95

Jazz Standards

Over 100 great jazz favorites: Ain't Misbehavin' • All of Me • Come Rain or Come Shine • Here's That Rainy Day • I'll Take Romance • Imagination • Li'l Darlin' • Manhattan • Moonglow • Moonlight in Vermont • A Night in Tunisia • The Party's Over • Solitude • Star Dust • and more.
00361407 . . . .$19.95

Latin Songs

80 hot Latin favorites, including: Amapola (Pretty Little Poppy) • Amor • Bésame Mucho (Kiss Me Much) • Blame It on the Bossa Nova • Feelings (¿Dime?) • Malagueña • Mambo No. 5 • Perfidia • Slightly out of Tune (Desafinado) • What a Diff'rence a Day Made • more.
00310689 . . . .$19.95

Love and Wedding Songbook

90 songs of devotion including: The Anniversary Waltz • Canon in D • Endless Love • Forever and Ever, Amen • Just the Way You Are • Love Me Tender • Sunrise, Sunset • Through the Years • Trumpet Voluntary • and more!
00361445 . . . .$19.95

Movie Music

73 favorites from the big screen, including: Can You Feel the Love Tonight • Chariots of Fire • Cruella De Vil • Driving Miss Daisy • Easter Parade • Forrest Gump • Moon River • That Thing You Do! • Viva Las Vegas • The Way We Were • When I Fall in Love • and more.
00310240 . . . .$18.95

Nostalgia Songs

100 great favorites from yesteryear, such as: Ain't We Got Fun? • Alexander's Ragtime Band • Casey Jones • Chicago • Danny Boy • Second Hand Rose • Swanee • Toot, Toot, Tootsie! • 'Way Down Yonder in New Orleans • The Yellow Rose of Texas • You Made Me Love You • and more!
00310730 . . . .$17.95

Rock 'N' Roll

100 classics, including: All Shook Up • Bye Bye Love • Duke of Earl • Gloria • Hello Mary Lou • It's My Party • Johnny B. Goode • The Loco-Motion • Lollipop • Surfin' U.S.A. • The Twist • Wooly Bully • Yakety Yak • and more.
00361411 . . . .$21.95

Singalong!

100 of the best-loved popular songs ever: Beer Barrel Polka • Crying in the Chapel • Edelweiss • Feelings • Five Foot Two, Eyes of Blue • For Me and My Gal • Indiana • It's a Small World • Que Sera, Sera • This Land Is Your Land • When Irish Eyes Are Smiling • and more.
00361418 . . . .$18.95

Standard Ballads

91 mellow masterpieces, including: Angel Eyes • Body and Soul • Darn That Dream • Day By Day • Easy to Love • Isn't It Romantic? • Misty • Mona Lisa • Moon River • My Funny Valentine • Smoke Gets in Your Eyes • When I Fall in Love • and more.
00310246 . . . .$19.95

Swing Standards

93 songs to get you swinging, including: Bandstand Boogie • Boogie Woogie Bugle Boy • Heart and Soul • How High the Moon • In the Mood • Moonglow • Satin Doll • Sentimental Journey • Witchcraft • and more.
00310245 . . . .$19.95

TV Themes

More than 90 themes from your favorite TV shows, including: The Addams Family Theme • Cleveland Rocks • Theme from Frasier • Happy Days • Love Boat Theme • Hey, Hey We're the Monkees • Nadia's Theme • Sesame Street Theme • Theme from Star Trek® • and more.
00310841 . . . .$19.95